Looking After Your Pet
Your Hamster

Written by
Rebecca Phillips-Bartlett

KidHaven
PUBLISHING

Published in 2026 by
KidHaven Publishing, an Imprint of
Greenhaven Publishing, LLC
2544 Clinton St., Buffalo, NY 14224

© 2025 BookLife Publishing Ltd.

Written by: Rebecca Phillips-Bartlett
Edited by: E.C. Andrews
Designed by: Amelia Harris

All facts, statistics, web addresses, and URLs in this book were verified as valid and accurate at time of writing. No responsibility for any changes to external websites or references can be accepted by either the author or publisher.

Cataloging-in-Publication Data
Names: Phillips-Bartlett, Rebecca.
Title: Your Hamster / Rebecca Phillips-Bartlett.
Description: Buffalo, NY : Kidhaven Publishing, 2026. | Series: Looking after your pet | Includes index and glossary
Identifiers: ISBN 9781534550667 (pbk) | ISBN 9781534550674 (library bound) | ISBN 9781534550681 (ebook)
Subjects: LCSH: Hamsters--Juvenile Literature | Pets—Juvenile Literature
Classification: LCC SF459.H3 P45 2026 | DDC 636.9356 --dc25

All rights reserved.

No part of this book may be reproduced in any form without permission in writing from the publisher, except by a reviewer.

Manufactured in the United States of America

CPSIA compliance information: Batch #CSKH26
For further information contact Greenhaven Publishing LLC at 1-844-317-7404.

Please visit our website,
www.greenhavenpublishing.com.
For a free color catalog of all our high-quality books, call toll free 1-844-317-7404 or fax 1-844-317-7405.

Find us on

Image Credits

Images are courtesy of Shutterstock.com. With thanks to Getty Images, Thinkstock Photo, and iStockphoto. Cover - Artishok, Petro Perutskyi, ZaZa Studio. Recurring Images - Victoria Nevzorova, Vladislav Lyutovm, itiir, ksuklein. 2-3 - Irina Vasilevskaia. 4-5 - New Africa, Hintau Aliaksei. 6-7 - MiViK, satoshinpi. 8-9 - Best dog photo, Seattle Roll, Happy monkey. 10-11 - Seattle Roll, Aimmi, Koko Foto, mahirart, Chatham172, the8monkey, Garna Zarina. 12-13 - Sabelskaya, Seattle Roll, Johannes Menge, GUNDAM_Ai. 14-15 - IRINA ORLOVA. 16-17 - Pixel-Shot, Tada Images. 18-19 - matteo fabbri, IgorAleks. 20-21 - eleonimages, satoshinpi. 22-23 - AlexKalashnikov, sabza, Vinicius R. Souza.

Contents

Page 4   A Perfect Pet
Page 6   Getting a Hamster
Page 8   Your Hamster's Home
Page 10   Diet
Page 12   Playtime
Page 14   Keeping Clean
Page 16   The Vet
Page 18   Settling In
Page 20   Fabulous Hamster Facts
Page 22   An Amazing Owner
Page 24   Glossary and Index

Words that look like this can be found in the glossary on page 24.

A Perfect Pet

Hamsters are known for their big, stretchy cheek pouches. These cute, funny little rodents make the perfect pets for many people. However, despite their tiny size, hamsters still need a lot of care.

Are you thinking about getting a hamster? This guide will help you decide whether a hamster is the perfect pet for you.

Even if you already have a hamster, it is important to keep learning more about their needs.

Getting a Hamster

Before getting a hamster, think about:

- How much space and quiet your hamster needs
- How much money caring for your hamster will cost, including toys, food, and vet care

Having a pet hamster is a big *responsibility*.

There are many different types of hamsters. Most hamsters must live alone. Before you get a hamster, check whether they can live with others. You can get hamsters from rescue centers, pet shops, and breeders.

Rescue centers give homes to animals in need.

Your Hamster's Home

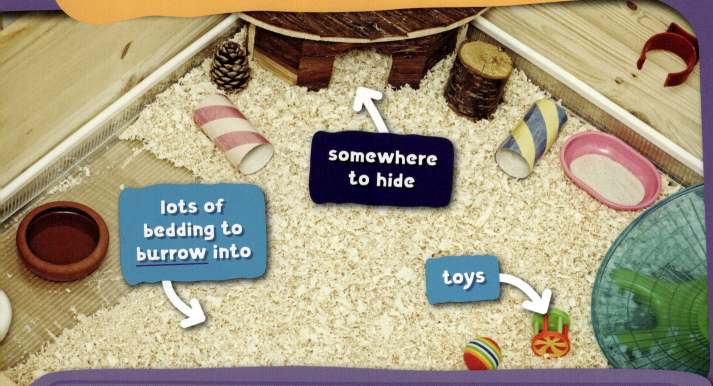

Pet hamsters love to run, so they need lots of space. Your hamster's cage should be at least 3 feet (1 m) long, 20 inches (50 cm) wide, and 20 inches (50 cm) tall.

Hamsters are nocturnal, which means they are most active at night. Your hamster's cage should be kept somewhere quiet so they can rest during the day. During the night, they might be noisy.

The lights in your hamster's room should go on and off at around the same time each day.

Diet

In the wild, hamsters eat seeds, cereals, and insects. Pet hamsters get most things they need from specially made hamster pellets. You can also give your hamster some seeds, fruits, vegetables, and mealworms as snacks.

Hamsters can carry lots of food in their cheek pouches.

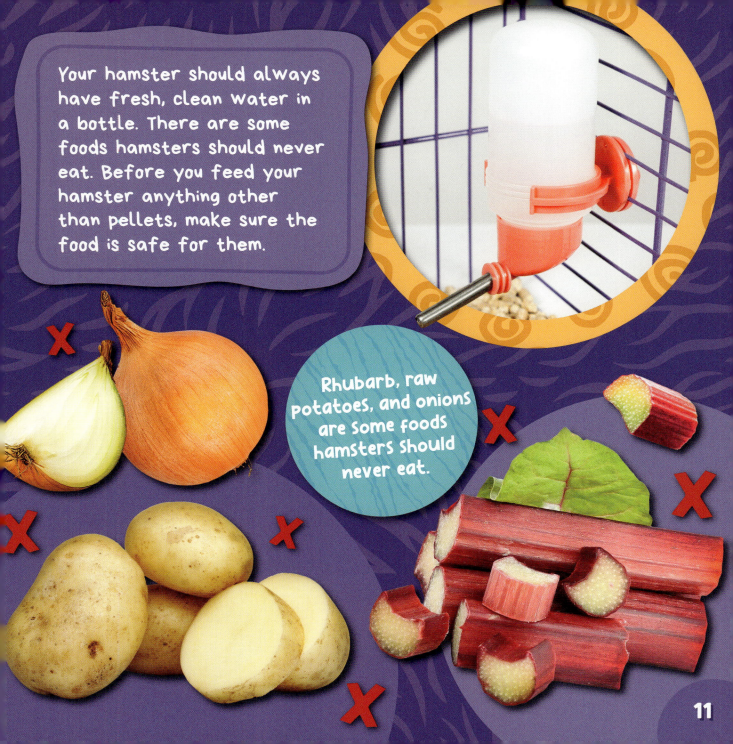

Your hamster should always have fresh, clean water in a bottle. There are some foods hamsters should never eat. Before you feed your hamster anything other than pellets, make sure the food is safe for them.

Rhubarb, raw potatoes, and onions are some foods hamsters should never eat.

Playtime

Hamsters are very shy animals. Imagine how scary everything would be if you were as tiny as a hamster! If you want to hold your pet hamster, you will need to be very gentle.

Head to page 18 to learn more about handling your hamster.

At night, your hamster will be full of energy. Hamster wheels are a great way for them to exercise. The wheel must be big enough for your hamster to run in without bending their back or lifting their head.

What could your hamster play with while you sleep?

Keeping Clean

Keeping your hamster's cage clean helps keep them healthy. Their cage should be cleaned every week. When you clean the cage, leave a handful of their old bedding inside so it still smells like home.

Any poop should be cleaned from the cage every day.

Hamsters mostly groom their own fur to keep themselves clean. However, some long-haired hamsters might need some brushing. Sand baths are a great way of helping your hamster look after their fur.

Always make sure the sand is safe for hamsters.

The Vet

Hamsters are sometimes known as exotic pets. Some vets do not treat small or exotic animals. Before you get a hamster, find out which vets near you can care for hamsters.

The vet is like a doctor for your pet.

Just like humans, hamsters can get sick. If you notice your hamster is acting differently or seems unwell, tell a grown-up right away. Your hamster can visit the vet to find out what is wrong.

Hamsters usually travel to the vet in small cages.

Settling In

Hamsters can get scared easily. It may take them a bit of time to feel settled and happy to be held. Hamsters may be more comfortable with grown-ups who are quiet and gentle but confident.

Never wake your hamster up. It might make them stressed.

When your hamster is ready to be held, open their cage. Hold out a treat, such as a seed or vegetable. Let them come to you. Keep quiet so they do not get scared.

Never open your hamster's cage without a grown-up.

Fabulous Hamster Facts

Hamsters are rodents. Rodents have front teeth that never stop growing. Most rodents gnaw on wood to stop their teeth from getting too long.

In the wild, hamsters run about 5 miles (8 km) every night. That is about as long as 80 soccer fields!

Hamsters do not have very good eyesight. They are color-blind and cannot see very far in front of themselves. When your hamster is out of their cage, make sure they do not fall off anything.

An Amazing Owner

Taking care of a hamster is a big responsibility. However, learning all about looking after a hamster is a great first step. Remember that every type of hamster is different.

You and a grown-up should learn everything you can about each type of hamster before bringing one home. Knowing all about hamsters will help you become an amazing owner to your new fluffy friend!

What would you name your hamster friend?

23

Glossary

breeders	people who bring animals together to make babies that they can sell
burrow	to dig a hole or tunnel
color-blind	unable to see certain colors
gnaw	bite, chew, or nibble a lot
responsibility	being in charge of doing something; doing the things that are supposed to be done
rodents	mammals, such as rats, mice, and squirrels, that have long front teeth which grow throughout their whole lives

Index

bedding 8, 14
bottles 11
cages 8–9, 14, 17, 19, 21
fur 15
grown-ups 17–19, 23
pellets 10–11
poop 14
rescue centers 7
rodents 4, 20
sand 15
vegetables 10, 19
wheels 13